simply COUNTRY

simply COUNTRY

creating comfortable style for cottage living

Liz Bauwens and Alexandra Campbell

photography by Simon Brown

CICO BOOKS

LONDON NEW YORK

Dedication

From Liz:

To my husband, Simon Brown, and my children,
Lois, Milo and Finn

From Alexandra:

To my husband, David Iron, and my children,
Freddie and Rosie

Published in 2007 by CICO Books
an imprint of Ryland Peters & Small Ltd
20–21 Jockey's Fields
London WC1R 4BW

10 9 8 7 6 5 4 3 2

A CIP catalogue record for this book is available from the British Library

ISBN-10: 1-9049-9188-2
ISBN-13: 978-1-9049-9188-5

Printed in China

Editor: Gillian Haslam
Designer: Christine Wood
Photographer: Simon Brown
Illustrator: Trina Dalziel
Project text: Jane Bolsover

CONTENTS

introduction

The words 'country home' evoke a sanctuary with roaring log fires, long walks and a chance to connect with nature. 'Country' as a decorating concept means easy, relaxed and pretty. While city houses stand for all that is smart and new, the country home is romantic, evocative and comfortable – a treasured scrap of vintage fabric, fresh blue-and-white stripes from the 20th century, an old wooden table or wicker chair brought out into the sunshine again – even a house's fixtures and fittings are re-used, re-painted or re-worked until they become part of a patchwork of memories.

This kind of country decorating – where everything has a use and nothing is thrown away unnecessarily – is especially relevant today now that everyone is concerned about consumerism and their carbon footprint. Much of the furniture on these pages has come from junk shops, flea markets, car-boot fairs and auctions, or has been handed down from friends and relatives. Each piece has a story, yet together it all looks fresh and contemporary.

Country homes can be grand mansions or humble cottages, modern houses or period styles. What they have in common is a sense of their roots through the use of local materials and craftsmanship. It is this, now that the same brands are to be found on every high street, that makes these interiors feel so special. There is a sense of individuality, cherished by those who live like this, following a code of 'always repair rather than replace'.

On these pages people have re-painted kitchen units, the sides of antique baths and old flooring; they have made their own rugs, adapted ends of fabric and vintage curtains – and achieved such stylish effects that glossy magazines clamour to feature their homes. And it's not difficult. As well as all the tips and advice throughout the pages on how to achieve these light-filled, airy interiors, at the end of the book there are ten projects to make which embody the spirit of the book.

'Country' stands for simplicity and welcome, fresh or faded florals, natural materials like cotton, wool, linen and stone, furniture with the patina of age and hand-painted china and pottery. And it's not expensive. By decorating in this way, you spend time, rather than money, creating a home that is stylish, comfortable and surprisingly in touch with a new direction in fashion.

Liz Bauwens and Alexandra Campbell

left: This house dates back to the 17th century, and every generation has left its mark. The cupboards, probably added during the 19th century, are too low for the proportions of the room, so the stencil above the doors adds height.

right: Here the cups, mirror frame and candlestick displayed on the mantelshelf are all in silver, producing a calm, unfussy look. You don't have to match items exactly but if you pick a common theme, antique and modern pieces will work well together.

CONTEMPORARY COUNTRY HOUSE

The grand country house, quintessentially a mix of old and new, has been revitalized for today's more casual lifestyles. It retains its beauty and sense of history, but is simpler, calmer and lighter.

left: The 'hood' above the range cooker was designed to hide ugly pipework. The weathervane on the countertop is a model of the racehorse, Dulcie Bella, whose winnings funded part of the Victorian building.

above and right: The kitchen units are a 'hotchpotch' – all different and free-standing, but pulled together into a unified look by painting them all cream, and the simple butler's sink suits the style perfectly.

A sense of history is at the heart of an authentic country look. Houses in cities follow fashion, with money always available to renovate and restore them completely. In the countryside, generations 'make do', using the materials to hand, adapting what they've got, always repairing rather than replacing, and only replacing when they must.

Samways Farm, a 17th-century Wiltshire farmhouse and one of the houses featured in this chapter, is a fine example of this style and ethos of decoration. The present owners were early advocates of decorating in this way, using traditional materials such as lime mortars and distemper wherever possible.

traditional decorating materials

It is difficult to date Samways Farm, but the building is an intriguing mix of original building and additions from the 17th, 18th and 19th centuries, and the owners have restored it with respect to its history, rather than gutting it of anything they didn't personally like. When they started out, it was difficult to source the distemper and lime plasters required for sympathetic renovation, but it is now widely recognized that using modern materials, such as cement or vinyl-based paints, in traditionally-built houses can, in fact, make damp

left: This four-poster bed is not dressed with traditional hangings, but looks light and modern when simply painted and strung with fairy lights. The proportions are right for the high-ceilinged room.

right: Paint – in soft, traditional colours – is at the heart of this bedroom. The French-style wardrobe, bedside tables, four-poster bed and floor are all painted with historic paints. Pattern is understated, with just a few delightful leaves embroidered on the bedspread, echoing the pattern on the small upholstered chair. See page 144 for instructions on making the embroidered bed throw.

problems worse. Lime and distemper allow houses to 'breathe', which means any damp problems will dry out easily.

The traditional-looking bathroom featured on these pages has been recently installed at Samways Farm, using a mixture of new and old fittings, hunted down in reclamation yards and junk shops and through local freesheets, while the walls are painted with distemper sourced from a traditional paint specialist (see page 158).

The key to this style of renovation is resist the temptation to gut a house immediately. Live with it first, while you consult historic societies and conservation specialists about how it should be treated. Only use builders, surveyors and craftsmen who genuinely understand historic buildings. Look for second-hand fittings in reputable salvage yards (see addresses on page 158) or seek out good-quality replicas. Cheap 'Victorian-style' mass-market fittings rarely look right – it is better to pick a simple, modern style instead.

above left: The claw-footed bath was bought through an advert in a local freesheet.

above: The brackets for this new basin came from a reclamation yard, and the cupboard is home-made.

right: This Victorian fireplace's dark wood was lightened with white paint. The light fitting reflected in the mirror dates from 1911 and is original to the farmhouse.

far left: Here you can just see the edge of 19th-century stencil 'wallpaper' which has been restored to its former glory.

left: This French candelabra was wired for electricity in three of its five arms. The remaining two have been left untouched so they can house candles.

right: A simple ivy garland looks good against the soft, natural effect of distemper paint.

In the upstairs hallway of Samways Farm, dark brown stencil 'wallpaper' dating from the 19th century (or possibly earlier) was uncovered when modern wallpaper was removed. It had been damaged in places, for example where electrical wires had been chased in, but the owners were able to restore it.

The bedroom featured here has been recently decorated with ivy for a wedding party (Samways Farm is also a bed-and-breakfast establishment as well as a home). Although the ivy is now dried out, it still looks just as attractive, especially with the French candelabra on the walls. These were originally for candles, but have now been wired for electric light. Only three arms have been wired as five electric bulbs would have been too bright. The iron bedstead is a traditional style, and it is easy to find either new or second-hand ones, although antique beds should always be given good-quality new mattresses.

The fireplace is a simple one, painted white like several others in the house. Fireplaces have now become almost a fashion item, with people ripping them out and replacing them with styles they prefer, but sometimes there is more charm and beauty in making the most of what you've got.

This bedroom has awkwardly shaped cupboards, so the owner decided to 'lose' them by painting them the same neutral shade as the walls. If you have fitted or architectural elements you don't like in a room, this is the most effective – and least expensive – way of minimizing their presence.

The paintings on the wall are by Katharine Armitage, and are hung traditionally from picture rails so their overall shapes echo the long lines of a mirror opposite (see next page). The predominantly soft colours of the furnishings are given punch and impact by the addition of a darker throw and the cushion on the chaise longue.

Using mirrors is a great way to create unexpected views of a room. Here light from the chandelier is enhanced by placing the chandelier in front of the mirror. Below it dangles a leftover Christmas decoration, scattering colour around the room. Think about the position of the mirror – it can be wonderful if placed to catch sight of a beautiful tree in the garden, for example, or the reflection of a favourite painting, but don't sit mirrors opposite each other as the effect is jarring. And you don't have to spend a great deal of money to get something that looks as if it belonged in a grand country house. Scour junk shops to find a mirror with the right dimensions for your room, or you could even buy something modern and give it an antique look by gilding the frame yourself (see page 157 for instructions).

Fabric, of course, plays a big part in the country-house look, and the best-loved palette is one of traditional patterns – often florals – which have faded over the years to soft, gentle, natural tones of pink, beige and green. It is often called the 'tea-stained' look, and it is a perennial favourite, never really going out of fashion. You can buy lovely faded florals from the top design houses, or try scouring attics and second-hand curtain shops. To achieve this look, try partnering different patterns in similar tones with cushions, curtains, cloths and upholstery.

At the fresher end of the palette are the toiles – soft pinks, blues and greens, often portrayed as floral patterns or scenes from country life in yesteryear, set on a white or cream background. These pretty, sometimes whimsical fabrics are perfect for country-house bedrooms and bathrooms and can help to add character to even the most modern of settings.

left: An inexpensive MDF dressing table, placed between windows dressed with damask curtains, has its humble origins disguised by a floor-length toile tablecloth (see pages 152–153 for instructions for making the cloth). A circle of glass, cut to order, sits on top of the cloth, protecting the top of the table. A matching footstool and semi-circular table have been dressed in similar cloths, bringing unity to the room.

right: A smaller room, like this bathroom, is an opportunity to use a grand material because you won't require much fabric. These curtains were bought second-hand – this is often an inexpensive way to buy curtains of this depth, and because they are designed to 'puddle' on the floor, you don't need to be so precise about their length.

Everything in this bathroom, including the wood panelling, has been painted a soft, historic white, creating the perfect backdrop for a collection of antique linen towels, hanging on the towel rail. As the window still has its original wooden shutters – and the room is quite small – curtains would be too much. However, to soften the look of a long thin window, a pretty fabric valance has been added (see page 151 for making instructions).

The little paintings hung around the bathroom add a personal touch. If pictures are properly framed, they're unlikely to be damaged by steam, and they don't have to be valuable. Try framing favourite postcards, illustrations from books or children's paintings.

living rooms

The country-house look has always been associated with chintzes and frills, but, in fact, the real key to it is reusing as much furniture, art and china as possible. Even in the grandest families, nothing was ever thrown out – it was tucked away in attics, cellars and empty rooms. When the next generation inherited the house, the new châtelaine would put away the things she didn't like, and rummage around to find and re-introduce treasures that had been rejected by previous inhabitants.

You can treat auction rooms, antique shops, junk shops and car-boot sales as your ancestral 'attic' to achieve the look, and your money will go so much further than if you buy everything new.

left and above: These straw hats are not just for display – they are on hand to be worn when going out in the garden in the hot sun.

right: The angel displayed on the mantelpiece was bought in an antique shop with a wing broken off, but it has been restored to full glory. The mirror was an inexpensive buy, but with dressing-gown cord gilded and draped over the top it looks far grander (see page 157 for instructions).

If you buy or inherit a grand country house, live with the rooms for a while before deciding which ones you really want or need to re-decorate. Because of their size, large country houses have always been re-decorated relatively rarely, and it's common to have paints and wallpapers that are up to a hundred years old.

New fabrics can make old paintwork look dirty and shabby, so collect and reuse fabrics – anything from old tablecloths to bedspreads and curtains – to cover chairs and sofas. Small pieces of fabrics can be made into cushion covers. The pink floral cover on the footstool featured here is actually an old duvet cover, which follows the Duchess of Devonshire's dictum that every room must have a '*coup de rouge*', roughly translated as a 'splash of red'. It has been lined and re-hemmed to give it some weight.

below: The pink fabric on this footstool is actually an old duvet cover, now enjoying a new lease of life.

right: The English country house look is relaxing and comfortable, with faded fabrics, easy chairs and layers of rugs.

There's a confidence about an English country house that partners a child's painting next to an Old Master, and displays a priceless heirloom beside a chipped vase. This mix of old and new, family and formal, top quality and everyday usage, is what gives the look its character and depth. There's no need to pay top money for perfection and big names – today you can buy fine-quality china with a few minor chips or an oil painting by an unknown artist really quite cheaply. Buy what you like, and forget about investment value. Only the very knowledgeable – or the exceptionally lucky – make money out of antiques.

In the rooms shown here, re-upholstering so much old furniture would have been punitively expensive and would have shown up the paintwork, so the sofas and chairs were covered with old fabrics. To recreate this look, try buying small pieces of expensive fabrics (usually available cheaply as offcuts in sales) to make a cushion or two, or take something much larger, like a curtain that is no longer fit to hang at a window, and use the good bits. Don't be constrained by what something is supposed to be – sheets, duvet covers, curtains and tablecloths can all be reworked very successfully.

left: The left-hand wall of the boot room is natural plaster which has been polished with beeswax. The rest of the room is painted in a shade to match.

below: The rough slate flagstones and soft grey paint on the woodwork run through the whole area. The worn slates add to the country atmosphere.

below right: Wooden African animals bring a sense of fun to the windowsill.

utility areas

The paintwork – stairways, skirting boards and door surrounds – of a grand country house is always practical, especially in what used to be the servants' areas, as re-painting miles of well-used corridors is rarely feasible, even for the greatest magnate. It's a lesson that we can all learn from. In the house shown here, all the paintwork is the same shade of soft grey, which goes well with both warm and cool colours. There is always a pot of paint readily available to touch up any damage, and dirty marks don't show up so much. It also feels very calm and serene to have the same colour used throughout the house, and, in smaller houses will make the space flow better.

This corridor, boot room and utility room show that such rooms don't have to be a mess. The soft pink on the walls gives the effect of the natural plaster and is both warm and light.

Even the newest modern house now has a utility room or area, and there's no reason why a practical area shouldn't look attractive as well. This is the flower room of a traditional English country house, but it is also blessed with lots of cupboards, now full of china for dinner parties, so doubles up as a purely practical storage space. A lovely old butler's sink and a display of favourite vases make it a pleasure to work in. As the room is quite dark, it's a perfect place for a watercolour – if hung in a bright room watercolours fade quickly.

left: Give your utility area that archetypal country house look with a butler's sink and practical, plain white tiles on the wall. Vases stored on shelves and windowsills look attractive and are readily available for use.

above: This jug, chosen for its shape and simplicity, has a timeless quality.

right: A darker room is an ideal place to protect a treasured watercolour by Lindy Guinness.

left: The traditional butler's sink is at the heart of the country kitchen look. Here it is partnered with a teak draining board and lots of white paint.

right: Kilner jars and tins from the 1940s and 50s provide attractive yet practical storage. You may need to replace the rubber seals on old glass storage jars.

NEW COTTAGE STYLE

Roses around the door, but just a simple blind at the window. Today's cottage style is easy, uncluttered and pretty, making the most of smaller rooms, vintage fabrics and 'objets trouvés'.

simplicity and texture

Cottage style doesn't have to mean frills and clutter. With its white paint, natural matting floor and inexpensive fabrics, this cottagey sitting room looks fresh and modern while being firmly rooted in traditional materials and local architecture. The fireplace looks good left as bare as this – while it would be a shame to rip out an architectural feature that belonged in the house, fireplaces in many houses have already gone, and uncovering them like this is as good (and sometimes better) than finding a replacement hearth.

The blind at the window is made from antique mattress ticking fabric. This is an approach which can be adopted for other soft furnishings – for example, if you have a much-loved set of curtains which are too worn to hang at the window, you can have them cut down and turned into cushion covers.

left: A comfortable armchair and sofa at the living room end of the cottage kitchen. If your fireplace has been removed by previous owners, you can still open up the original hole for a delightful rustic effect.

right: Dark furniture, such as this lovely dining table, looks particularly effective against pale walls and clean lines. It allows it to be the star of the show. The blind at the window is made from antique mattress ticking, and, along with the floral pinafore, comes from Sharland & Lewis.

You don't need to associate country or cottage style with fiddly, twiddly woodwork. This kitchen is sleek and contemporary, with its smart wood worktop and long, modern door handles, yet it fits perfectly in a period building – whether it be a castle or a cottage – because it is so simple. There are just a few cottage-style touches – the checked enamel splashback behind the stove, the traditional clock on the wall and a long wooden pew under the window.

This is a long view of the kitchen shown on the previous page and it demonstrates just how well a simple, modern design can work with the soft squashy sofas and rustic checks of country style. A fitted kitchen is an expensive element in any house, so you don't really want to choose anything too extreme – for example, if you ever sell the house it may deter potential buyers. Cream walls, white units and a plain wooden worktop will work with every kind of interior, and you can have fun with the aspects that are easy to change, such as the china, accessories, soft furnishings and furniture.

Most of the furniture and accessories shown in these pictures are what could be termed 'modern antiques'. They date from the 20th century, usually from between the 1920s and the 1970s, and are relatively affordable and easy to find. Shops specializing in this era, such as Sharland & Lewis, show what can be done with such items, but you can also train your own eye by looking around auction rooms and junk shops. Some 20th-century designs are still being manufactured and are available in kitchen shops, or originals may be available via the Internet. The three bar stools shown below demonstrate how different styles can work well together (see pages 154–155 for instructions on re-covering the cushion).

right: In this country kitchen, the sink and units on either side were built by the owner's father, and, with their rounded handles and soft cream paint, their colour and detail is in keeping with the china collection. If you're adding units (or big items like a fridge) to a kitchen where everything is on display, think about the style of your china and glass. Here, the colour of one wall – a pretty mint green – also echoes the predominant colour in the collections.

below: The humble clothes peg has become a classic style icon, especially in bleached unpainted wood.

Some of the simplest domestic items have become design icons today. Blue-and-white striped Cornishware pottery, big enamel colanders, cream earthenware mixing bowls and other kitchen basics have been manufactured for over a hundred years and still look as good today as they did when they were first sold. You could use them anywhere – in a country cottage, of course, but also in a city loft apartment or a family home in the suburbs. Such pieces are not expensive and they are easy to find – and in a world where almost every charity shop uses specialist valuers to make sure that donations are valued realistically, kitchenware is still very affordable. And it's often stocked in chain stores too. Look for classic, simple shapes, colours you really love and charming, simple patterns. On this table, set for tea, are a traditional-style teapot and butter dish, plus a pair of pretty patterned 'chintz' cups, all to be found on almost any high street at any time in the last fifty years.

Simple cottage style is based on soft colours, stripes and checks, with no unnecessary frills or fuss, and this room – the dining end of the kitchen in the weekend retreat of florist Jane Packer – is a perfect example. Green is a natural choice for a florist, perhaps, and here her florist's eye for colour is evident in the way she's furnished everything in a limited palette of soft blues and greens, with patterns mainly in faded checks or stripes. This discipline is almost invisible, but it keeps the look uncluttered and yet relaxed, and means you can have quite a lot of things in a small space without it looking untidy.

Jane's favourite era for china, fabric and cookware is the 1930s and 40s, and she collects tablecloths, teapots, enamel and storage jars from this period, interspersed with pieces that are actually modern but have much the same feel. Once you choose a theme or colour that you like, it's easy to mix junk shop finds with cheap chain-store purchases, add in the odd expensive treat and make it all look as if it belongs together. And if you break a glass or a cup, you haven't spoilt a set.

left: Stripes and checks, blues and greens – it's a harmonious formula that's easy to achieve. The traditional shapes of china and cookware have stood the test of time and have become modern classics.

above right: Old-fashioned lights bought in an antique shop and rewired.

right: The enamel colander and other cookware are styles that have been around for at least a hundred years – search for them in junk shops or look for modern versions available in cookshops today.

new country bathrooms

When planning a bathroom you can mix traditional and modern fittings to great effect. This is, after all, exactly what would have happened in the past in cottages – some elements would have been recycled and others bought new. Here a conventional WC and built-in bath sit happily with a contemporary square washbasin and recycled tiles. The built-in wall of the shower gives a much more comfortable, solid feel than relying on plastic shower cubicles.

left and above: An attractive mix of traditional and contemporary bathroom fittings. You don't have to match basins, baths and WCs, and it is much more in keeping with a relaxed country style if you don't. A pretty mirror makes a delightful alternative to the now conventional fitted mirror glass.

This blue-tiled bathroom is tucked into the eaves of a cottage roof, a good way of finding a little extra space in a house. Here the skylight was increased in size to make the room lighter, but this would be unlikely to be an option if your house is listed or in a conservation area. You do need to consult your conservation officer if you add a bathroom to a listed building – many people don't realize that 'listed' doesn't just apply to the outside of a house, it also covers everything permanent inside, including the plumbing. If you add bathrooms to period houses without checking this, you could have difficulties when you come to sell.

above: Here a second bathroom has been squeezed into a roof space. Check planning regulations before installing a skylight.

right: The fabric used in this window blind is very cottagey, but it is more traditionally associated with curtains. Turning it into a blind brings cottage style up to date (see pages 146–147 for making instructions).

left: Here a 1970s chair is given a new lease of life by its unexpectedly romantic covering of rosy flowers, while plain linen curtains have been edged with vintage fabric – a good trick for making a small amount of lovely fabric go further (see page 150 for instructions).

right: Use flowers from the garden for the real country look – you only need two or three blooms casually arranged. If your garden doesn't have enough roses to be cut for indoor display, add shop-bought flowers to generous amounts of garden greenery.

CHECKS AND ROSES

Country patterns – checks, stripes and roses – are timeless and classic, and suit every property, from cottages to castles. The key to a contemporary look is not to overdo it – make one print a focus for a room or use a subtle palette of faded colour for a natural feel.

floral dining

This room is a traditional country-house dining room and was originally painted a heavy red. The first principle of this understated decoration is that one thing in the room needs to stand out, while everything else provides a quiet background. Here the strong, dark shapes of the 18th-century Chippendale-period chairs and the elegant outlines of the sconces provide the main statement, while the wall is now painted a soft pink and the dark, heavy dining table is covered with a cloth. The owner searched for the right wallpaper, but couldn't find it, so she painted one herself. She took some time to decide on the rose design, then painted two roses every evening after work, joining them up with a delicate blue ribbon. The contrast of the quiet, pretty walls and the dramatic chair backs is very successful.

left: The freehand pattern of roses painted on a plaster-pink wall was used to help lighten the traditionally heavy, masculine dining room.

below: The pretty rose-handled doorknob and fingerplate are original to the house, but similar ones can easily be bought from many home-style shops.

below right and right: The candles in the wall sconces are lit at night and create a festive twinkle. The little strings of balls dangling from them are inexpensive decorations, but they add a fun touch.

left: Layer and mix china and glass, combining ornate plates with plain designs. Good glass – listen for a high-pitched 'ting!' when you tap the rim gently – can be surprisingly cheap if bought in ones and twos. You can mix antique and new glass, or plain with cut.

below: Magnolia blooms displayed in an antique soup tureen. If you have an ornate vase, keep the flowers simple for a modern look, or marry a plain container with more striking blooms. This way, neither overwhelms the other.

mixing antique fabrics

There are two contemporary approaches to using floral designs: either allow one floral design to 'sing' amongst plain and textured fabrics, as seen below on this rosy chaise longue, or, as seen on the right, combine several muted patterns and textures. With the latter, consider the balance. Most patterns here are in similar faded colours and tones, with just a couple of cushions in a stronger accent colour. Or mix patterns – checks, stripes and florals – with a repeated colour theme.

below and right: Two different approaches to decorating with florals: a punchy Cath Kidston floral fabric is a focal point against a muted background, while on the right you can see how a combination of florals works together well if the patterns are mostly all the same tone, with a few cushions in darker or stronger 'highlight' colours to add depth.

left and above: A tablecloth keeps this palette of colours soft and neutral, and taking the cloth down to floor level means fewer furniture legs on view, and therefore a less cluttered look. The radiators are concealed with a pretty window seat.

In this elegant room, the mix of pattern and colour works well because it is so soft and understated, and there is plenty of plain fabric and paint to act as a foil for the gentle pattern. The big items – the curtains – are neutral, dressed with only a pair of simple rope tie-backs and no pelmet. All the pattern and colour are to be found in the smaller items, which are easy to change or update: the tablecloth, the window-seat cushions and the loose cover on the small armchair. Almost any pretty fabric works – here, the window-seat cushions have been patched with a tiny scrap of another floral fabric, all adding to the appeal.

classic country bathrooms

This bathroom in Samways Farm is the epitome of a grand English country-house bathroom, but is actually a mix of old and new. The strong pattern of the lino check floor draws together the dark and light elements: the delicate curtains, the pastel eiderdown draped over the chair, then the dark fireplace and protective lead flooring under the bath.

The WC is a modern one, but fitted with an antique seat and cistern. It looks as if it had been there for years. In fact, it was newly installed – it's easy to find old-fashioned overhead cisterns in reclamation yards. Choose yards that subscribe to the SALVO code (see page 158) to ensure that goods have not been stolen from other houses.

above: Checks always work well with florals: here a graphic black-and-white check floor makes a classic backdrop for delicate contemporary print curtains and a faded vintage eiderdown.

right: If there's too much white in a bathroom, you can paint the side of the bath. You don't need to use a specialist paint for revamping the outer sides of the bath.

The key to mixing different patterns and achieving a contemporary look is to work with a simple theme, adding lots of white, cream or neutral shades. Here the theme is pink, repeated in checks, flowers, patchwork and towels, but it never becomes cloying because the room itself is essentially pale, plain and neutral. The combination of cottagey old beams and a chandelier is a particularly nice touch – don't be afraid to juxtapose two very unlikely elements together.

flowers and glass

Flowers have a particular affinity with glass, as the clarity of the glass doesn't distract from their fragile beauty in the same way that patterned or coloured china does. Here we see two uses of glass and flowers – the first is the conventional glass vase of flowers, while the

left: Country-flower arrangements don't have to be complex compositions – nothing beats a simple glass vase with a handful of blooms. In the background are a couple of cut-glass decanters, now only used as decoration. The splash of colour from the flowers complements their sparkle delightfully.

second is the use of glass to protect a floral fabric used as a dresser top. In both these pictures, the flowers or the floral pattern are accompanied by several different kinds of glass in a 'still-life' composition – cut-glass decanters, a glass perfume bottle and a couple of glass mirrors. If you have collections of glass you want to display, adding a floral touch like this will give the grouping a lift.

right: This is a lovely way to use a scrap of precious fabric. Fold or sew it to the right size for a table top or the top of a chest of drawers, then protect it with a piece of glass cut to fit. It's a particularly effective way of enjoying a piece of antique fabric that is too delicate to make cushions with, and can be adapted for almost any piece of furniture, from coffee tables to dresser tops.

left: Almost everything in this room is second-hand in some way – either a junk shop find, like this pewter jug, or recycled from an earlier home, such as the fruitwood gate-leg table, which was handed down. There are a few new items, but they are simple and practical, like the free-standing reading light.

right: Instead of ornaments, create displays from collections of found objects, such as pebbles, driftwood and shells gathered on long walks.

MODERN RUSTIC

A simple, economical look, emphasizing the shapes and colours of beautiful everyday objects in pottery, wood and tin. Recycle – attics, junk shops and hand-me-downs are the key to this look.

left and above: A junk shop jug with dried flowers from the hedgerows, plus decorative plates of shells and seaweed. The more you look, the more you find: the days of discovering Old Masters in junk shops, for example, are over, because everyone now knows what things are worth, but if you develop your own style, and keep looking, you will find items that other people miss.

Country walks or strolls through market towns can be a great source of decorative objects for the modern rustic look. Whether you're scouring junk shops, walking along the beach or enjoying the beauty of the hedgerows, the principles are the same – get your eye in by looking whenever you get the chance. You might only see something you want to take home every so often, but the more you look, the more you will see. It also helps to have a theme – jugs, soda siphons, pebbles, shells, Shelley pottery… it doesn't matter what it is as long as you like it. Some people even put a price limit and this also focuses the mind. You might occasionally go over your limit, but only for something you really wanted.

Unfashionability can keep prices low, especially at auctions, and second-hand furniture is often relatively cheap, mainly because there is so much good furniture available to buy new at reasonable prices. Everyday wooden furniture from the 20th century is certainly worth buying, and you can paint or strip it if you wish. Visit an auction room and sit through an auction before bidding for the first time and, above all, establish what price you are prepared to pay for something and stick to it.

You don't need to have a sofa to create a cosy, comfortable sitting room. Here, two old leather armchairs are partnered with a new armchair upholstered in a check fabric. The Welsh blankets were all second-hand bargain buys – people forget that hunting around at car-boot sales and in junk shops can often reveal a few fabrics and soft furnishings tucked away, and that a bit of darning and a dry clean can work wonders. You can recognize a good wool blanket by the feel, and it's also worth getting to know which labels you like and looking out for them in particular.

recycle as much as you can

It has become almost standard practice to replace a kitchen today, but it really is worth looking at what you can do with what you've got rather than tearing out perfectly serviceable cabinets. Most surfaces can be re-painted, although you will sometimes need to use specialist base coats. Even a cheap plastic sink only needs bleach to bring back its sparkle.

In this kitchen, the owners painted the ceiling white and the floor blue, but they left the beams in their own natural wood colour. Many people think beams should be stained black, but, traditionally, all wood in cottages was either limewashed or left in its natural state.

above: This metal bread bin has been re-painted to cover up chips and then stencilled.

left: A fresh coat of paint has revitalized a dark kitchen. With walls, ceiling and kitchen units all painted the same shade of white and the floor painted blue, the space is immediately opened up.

right: Keeping colours simple also helps to keep the look light and airy – here the kitchen's blue floor and white walls are echoed in an old enamel teapot and some French china storage jars, both sourced from junk shops.

The wooden pew in this kitchen came as part of the fixtures and fittings when the present owners bought the cottage and it fitted their old French table perfectly. The cane chairs are probably French and are junk-shop finds, as is the tin lampshade, roughly painted an attractive shade of yellow. The weathered patina is part of its attraction. The paintings by Julia Dickens, propped up behind the pew, continue the kitchen theme and echo the fruit on the table. See page 156 for instructions for making the unusual cork teapot stand, seen here on the worktop.

the rustic bedroom

This cottage bedroom has a real feeling of space and light, with a white-painted floor, walls and ceiling. Painting floorboards white always brightens a room, and you can use yacht varnish and specialist floor paints for a hard-wearing finish.

The chest and rows of hooks provide simple yet adequate storage. Using hooks rather than cupboards is a traditional cottage habit, as they take up less space than a conventional wardrobe. You can't, admittedly, keep as much on a row of hooks as you can in a cupboard, but an increasing number of people today now divide their storage into short and long term, keeping only clothes they are currently using in their bedrooms and storing last season's clothes. The white chest is a shop fitting, and it isn't old. It's typical of the kind of thing you can now find in second-hand shops, as it doesn't have any real value – it just looks good, and all this one needed was cleaning up.

far left: A few branches of tree blossom make a simple and dramatic floral statement, in keeping with the cottage style.

left: A row of metal hooks replaces cupboard storage.

right: White-painted floors create a holiday feel and lighten a room. Today's floor paints are hard-wearing, but it's also worth accepting a certain amount of wear and tear as part of the charm of the look. The chest is a second-hand shop fitting.

The bed is the main decoration in this pretty little room. If you're faced with a small room, keep it simple, and don't forget about comfort. Here a double bed – as large as the room can hold – takes up most of the space at this end of the room. A plain blind replaces curtains, and there are no pictures on the wall, while at the other end of the room there is a chest, plus hooks for hanging clothes (see previous pages). Apart from the bedding, everything – floor, walls, bed frame, light shade and chest – is white.

On the bed, an attractive crocheted coverlet introduces all the colour the room needs, and it means you can vary the feel, perhaps with a rose-print eiderdown or a patchwork quilt. Crochet – with all its craft connotations – is a very 'modern rustic' fabric, and it is something that is relatively easy to learn yourself. Or you can buy it – look out for craft fairs and local craft sales.

You can also buy quilting kits with fabric squares cut to size so that you can make your own patchwork quilt by stitching them how you like.

left: A big bed in a small room is cosy, comfortable and cottagey. You hardly need anything else, but the crochet bedspread adds a vibrant splash of colour.

above: The same simple white glass lampshade is used in the central light fittings in all the bedrooms – it is pretty without being intrusive.

right: You can pick up little tables or stools to use as bedside tables in any junk shop. You don't always have to paint them – leaving them weathered and peeling adds to their country character.

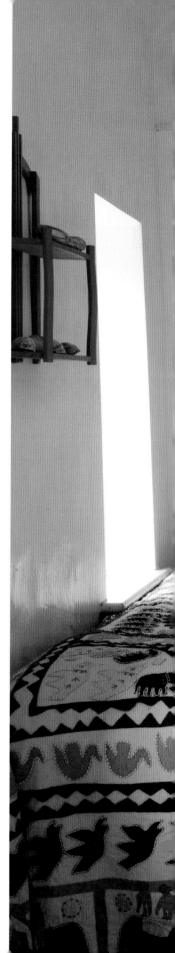

above and right: An Indian bedspread, with its folk-art shapes and strong colours, and a watercolour by Julia Dickens are the focal points of this bedroom. Everything else is painted white, although the bare brick emphasizes the shape of the chimney breast and adds a touch of warmth. Note the tongue-and-groove door and iron latches, which are common to most old cottages. If this kind of detail has been removed by previous owners, it is always worth replacing.

left: A tiny single room with a wrought-iron bed. But it's not a Victorian original – it was bought many years ago at a modern furniture store, and the patchwork quilt is contemporary too. The little wicker chest is typical of the kind of thing available in most junk shops today. It was actually a washing-basket, so you can take the lid off. It was painted a soft, distressed blue.

above right: An odd china cup missing its saucer can be used as a vase.

right: Old baths like this can be re-conditioned. Hiding the pipework behind tongue-and-groove boarding looks good and the cupboard doors next to it mean there is easy access if the plumbing requires maintenance.

left: Shelves filled with a collection of pretty 1930s, 40s and 50s china, grouped by colour. Colin the cat enjoys a snooze on mismatched patchwork cushions and a vibrant crazy patchwork quilt.

right: These kitchen units date from the building's institutional use in the 1960s, but instead of replacing them, the owner painted everything – even the dishwasher – a pretty shade of blue. An expert tip – try adding a tube of artist's Paynes Grey to calm a blue paint down (use watercolour artist's paint in water-based house paints and artist's oil paint for oil-based formulae).

COUNTRY WHITES, COUNTRY COLOUR

Try decorating in soft whites and blues for a fresh-air feel, choose primitive patterns and brilliant hues for impact, or pick gently faded flower tones for the English country garden effect.

cream, white and blue

This is one of the classic country combinations – the cream of the dairy mixed with sky blues and splashes of white. This room forms the ground floor of a seaside home and the colours reflect the outside environment. It is an exceptionally big space so colour has been used to break up the vast expanses of wall – cream up to the point where there might otherwise have been a ceiling, white in the roof space and blue to pick out features such as the staircase and the door. Even the linoleum floor is painted white (using ordinary floor paint) but as it, too, is such a large area the owner has broken it up with small hand-painted diamond squares. It is reasonably hard-wearing but does require re-painting around once a year. The massive Swedish stove was bought second-hand from a café – it gave out far too much heat for a small room, but here in winter it is a great help at warding off the winds which blow straight off the sea.

The giant tables were once used for adult-education classes, and the big circular overhead lights are also second-hand. They double up as heaters, although this function has never been wired up, and indeed there doesn't seem much point in heating the roof space.

below left: A blue-painted table bought from an adult-education centre is used to display two quirky statuettes.

below: The floral panels on the bench were hand-painted. The peeling paint adds to its charm.

right: Second-hand patchwork quilts and tablecloths mean that no-one has to worry much about spilling things. The white chair covers keep the look fresh and airy, and they can easily be laundered.

This kitchen is almost unchanged in layout since it was used by a children's charity as a seaside holiday home decades ago. Even the stove, grill and long table date back to those times. A coat of blue paint and two massive model yachts plus some new blue linoleum on the floor have transformed it at a fraction of the cost of installing a new kitchen. On the mantelpiece there is a line of standard catering glass salt and pepper cellars – used by the children of 30 years ago and still very useful for parties!

Blue-and-white is probably the most classic and timeless country combination of all. It always looks fresh, and is very easy to achieve. Add in a splash of pink or red to prevent it from looking too cold – here the warmer colours are seen in the flowers on the rug and cushions.

The glass-fronted cabinets were picked up in a second-hand shop, but many of today's homeware chains sell similar items which you could paint. They make excellent display cases for anything valuable or likely to break. The whole unit on the wall is hung like a big picture, visually linked to the sofa below.

The rug in front of the sofa is actually a floor cloth, made by artist Marilyn Phipps. She simply buys pieces of artist's canvas, cut to size, and paints on them, although the less artistic could use stencils to achieve a similar effect. This is an easy way to create a mat in the perfect colours to match other elements in the room.

The wooden chest, with its shallow wide drawers, would originally have been used as storage for architect's plans. Most chests like this are plain varnished wood, but when painted white and decorated with a delicate leaf motif, this one becomes a much lighter piece and suitable for a living area. A fun collection of old-fashioned painted wooden toys completes the picture.

left: A blue-and-white striped fabric on the sofa gives it a casual feel, while the rosy cushions prevent the blue from looking cold. The 'rug' is a piece of artist's canvas, hand-painted and cut to size.

above right: An antique child's painted toy – a wooden Noah's ark – makes a charming ornament on the window ledge.

right: An architect's plan chest, painted white and decorated with a leaf motif. Note that it is a slightly different white from the walls – there are many shades of white to choose from and using different shades helps to prevent the room looking stark or cold.

These two bedrooms, both in the same house, show contrasting approaches to decoration. The bedroom below is painted white and is free of clutter, while the natural pine room is 'crowded up' with pictures and souvenirs. Both rooms are charming, and it is interesting to note that both styles – the minimalist and the maximalist – probably have more impact than simply placing just one or two pictures on each wall. The choice is entirely up to you and your taste.

The wall full of mementoes, seen on the right, has a seaside theme, complementing the location of this beach-side house, and the pictures are framed in natural wood to match the walls, but otherwise there are no rules. The bare, monk-like room, with its light, white walls, makes the most of the pretty bedspreads and painted bedheads. White is a particularly good choice for very bare rooms – it makes the most of the light and space and is quite a statement. The warm wood walls, on the other hand, might have felt a bit too much like a sauna if they had been left bare.

left: A simply painted white room is left almost bare, except for painted bedheads and pretty charity-shop quilts.

right: The collections on the wall have a general seaside theme, and the picture frames are also wood – but otherwise this is an instinctive, anything-goes approach and a great way of displaying things that remind you of someone or something special.

blues and greens

These pictures show blues and greens working together in fairly bright mid-tones. There used to be a saying that 'blue and green should never be seen/without a colour in between.' It is completely untrue. Some of the harsher blue and green dyes of the mid-20th century did jangle together, but in fact green is partly composed of blue (the other primary colour in green, as every school child knows, is yellow). In a colour wheel blue is close to green, and colours that follow each other make a particularly harmonious combination. Throw in a splash of red or pink, as an accent colour.

Greens and blues are also considered to have soothing, anti-depressive effects on the brain, according to colour therapy. Blue is widely considered a spiritual colour, while green has become the colour of ecology and the signal to 'go ahead'. This makes a blue-green combination particularly appropriate for the country.

left: Green is the classic country colour, but it looks fresh and modern in this slightly acid-green tone. Coloured glass is always fun and you can mix different shades together.

right: This dresser was in a very dark wood, so it was given a new lease of life when it was painted in a spring-like green. Dark furniture is out of fashion at the moment, so it can be picked up relatively cheaply, then transformed into something new for just the cost of a coat of paint. It can always be stripped and re-varnished again if fashions change.

white and bright colours

White interiors can be soothing and harmonious, as seen in the 'vintage whites' feature on pages 110–115, but as shown here, they can also make great backgrounds for bright, primitive colour – brilliant reds, greens, blues, yellows and pinks. The white used on these pages, however, is a 'soft' white – one of the many 'quieter' shades of white now available from many paint manufacturers. Therefore, rather than opting for a basic brilliant white, try out sample pots of softer whites to see which ones complement the more vibrant soft furnishings you wish to use in the room.

left: This orange-and-blue knitted cotton blanket comes from Stitch Designworks, a mail-order company that sources and commissions home fabrics and knitwear from all around the world.

right: Brightly coloured peasant-style plates and a vivid red-and-yellow Hawaiian-print fabric from the same mail-order company on a footstool make this country kitchen an uplifting and welcoming place to be. The fabric is simply staple-gunned to the framework, making it very easy to change if you want to give the room a different look.

left: Wipeable whiteboard wallpaper, written on with dry marker pens, provides a fun backdrop to the bright Hawaiian print from Stitch Designworks. The sofas have washable covers, which means you can still have white sofas when your house is populated by children and pets.

above left: Hobbs the kitten.

above centre: Old and new – the floral cushion is a Kaffe Fassett design. The rich floral looks fresh and modern beside a contemporary stripey cushion.

above right: This white chair with its colourful seat is one of Stitch Designworks' designs. The seat pops out so that you can change the seat cover as easily as putting on a new sweater.

This particular scheme is sunny, with punchy yellows, reds and oranges, but next week you could easily change the look and use a completely different range of colours. Cushions and throws are, of course, easy to switch around, and the white-painted chair has a seat which lifts out so that the covers can be changed whenever you feel like it. This is the beauty of keeping walls and floors white – they provide the perfect blank canvas when the look of the room needs a change of pace.

The wall is covered in whiteboard paper, and it can be written on with dry marker pen, then wiped off when the message is no longer needed.

When decorating with brilliant colours, keep tone in mind. All the colours in these rooms have a roughly similar depth or richness and this is partly why they work together. A peachy pastel would – probably – look out of place in the mix. But when experimenting with different looks is this easy, there's no harm in trying out unusual colour combinations.

colourful kitchens and dining

left and above: Splashes of bright colour, provided by kitchen equipment, fabrics and tiles, bring a welcoming warmth to a country kitchen.

Here, colour is provided by the china on display, along with the plain blue tiles behind the Aga, which will go with almost anything. Detail is the key: the unit handles came from a professional kitchen supplier's catalogue and the bar stools from the US. Design classics such as a Kitchenmaid coffee machine and Dualit toaster are on display. Old and new cookware in stainless steel looks good together.

Whether you live in the country or in an urban area, a conservatory is the most effective way of enjoying your garden all year round, and over the last couple of decades an unprecedented number of conservatories have been added to homes, many of them in the Victorian style seen here. Sometimes such conservatories don't feel as if they really belonged to the house but you can draw them in with a few simple changes.

Consider the flooring first, especially if you want to smarten it up or make it look more contemporary. This conservatory originally had red terracotta tiles, but they were changed for pale brick tiles which now run throughout an adjacent kitchen-living room, thus linking the conservatory visually with the main house. The door to the conservatory had also been a normal size, but by widening the opening it draws the two living areas together into one huge living space. Conservatory furniture has tended to focus on wicker and bamboo, but as this stylish conservatory-dining room with its American diner chairs shows, you can choose as wide a range of styles as in any other room. Furnish it the way you would the rest of your house, rather than letting it appear an afterthought.

There are two major things to bear in mind. Firstly, with so much sunlight, a conservatory can take bright colours better than any other room and, secondly, things will fade quite quickly in that sunlight. Often that makes them twice as nice, but if anything is really precious (for example, a watercolour painting), then the conservatory is not the place to hang it. The sunlight can dry fine furniture out too, so protect your dining table with a bright cloth.

above right: Gingham napkins with a coloured lace edge from Stitch Designworks (page 145 shows how to make similar ones).

right: The vibrant colours of the tablecloth are echoed in the flowers.

far right: American diner chairs, with their plastic seats, are stylish and wipeable. Try auction rooms, the Internet or antique shops. Mix high-street purchases, antiques and designer names for a contemporary look.

bedrooms and bathrooms

In the bedroom the bed is the dominant piece of furniture. This gives you the option to change colours and themes within the room by using different bedlinen. Here, there is also a contemporary use of fabric on the walls, and the bright Marimekko panels in the alcoves can be lifted out and changed. Lengths of wallpaper, mounted onto wooden batons, can create similar bold displays. Bedlinen in bright reds, pinks and whites continues the colour theme.

left: Although colours usually work best together when they are of a similar tone, such as the bright contrasting reds and yellows here, you can also work a very successful scheme by picking a range of tones within one colour. Here the two techniques have been combined: soft pinks with bright and deep reds, then the strong red with an equally vibrant shade of yellow in the throw from Stitch Designworks.

right: In the alcoves on either side of the bed are tall fabric panels which can easily be lifted out and changed.

White is also a colour choice, and is a light, peaceful backdrop. It also has the maximum flexibility – you can jazz it up with peasant-style primary colours, give it a patina with faded florals and checks – or make any number of other choices. A bathroom like this – simple, airy and white – can take literally any styling, whether it be modern towels and pictures or a traditional look. Here the detail – the taps, shower head, plain glass door and white tiling – is sleek and modern, but not obtrusively so and colour is minimal with just a few pretty towels. However, the plain cotton duck curtains could be swapped for anything from a traditional chintz to a modern print. More colour could be added with pictures on the walls – with a scheme this simple and elegant, your possibilities are unlimited.

below: A pretty country chintz draped over an old wooden chair looks fresh and attractive in a contemporary context.

right: The simplicity of this bathroom scheme means that it is peaceful, but also flexible enough to take more colour and pattern.

Soft pale pink is one of the most flexible and forgiving colours of all. It is both light and warm, and only fell out of fashion when 'magnolia' became a decorating cliché. This pink-washed room on the right has very little natural light but still looks light, sunny and beautiful when painted a gentle shade of plaster pink.

left: One of the great pleasures of decorating with wood is that you can paint it relatively easily. Here tongue-and-groove walls fitted with a peg rail, a wooden bedhead and a wooden bedside table are painted in a welcoming combination of pink and white, with contrasting mint green bedspread.

right: This was a dark, cluttered junk room until it was cleared out and painted a delicate shade of pink. Such a colour would work well in almost any situation, regardless of a room's natural light. Make sure you choose a shade that is not too sweet.

vintage whites

There are so many shades of white, from modern brilliant whites made with optical brighteners to softer standard whites, 'old' whites and whites with a hint of pink, grey or cream. This kitchen is made by kitchen and furniture designer, Nick Kenny from recycled cabinets, leftover tiles and junk-shop finds. Full of eclectic objects and things which have been picked up for little or no expense at all, it is drawn together with soft historic white paint and the use of weathered zinc.

Using white is a great way of opening up a space or making a room seem lighter, but it's worth experimenting with different shades to see which works best in any particular setting.

above and right: Designer Nick Kenny uses zinc recycled from Parisian rooftops on cupboard door fronts, kitchen worktops and even as 'pictures'. White furniture covers and gallons of white paint pull together a diverse collection of furniture perfectly.

Everything in this kitchen
is recycled and bought on a
tight budget, even the industrial
circular iron staircase (now
painted white) which was
bought on the Internet and
welded in place by a local boat-
builder. The tiles are leftovers,
hence the charming patchwork
effect, but because they are
all white, they work together.
The floor is made from
moisture-resistant chipboard –
painted white, of course –
and the blue-painted table
and woodwork around the
windows add a splash of colour.

This church was originally supplied as a corrugated iron flat-pack, delivered to the local station, then erected and lined with pine boards in 1870. After it was deconsecrated in 1950, it became a scout hall and then subsequently a camping shop and a joinery workshop, but has now been converted into a home.

The living area is full of an eclectic mix of items picked up from car-boot fairs and auctions, but with everything painted white, or draped with white covers, it all looks as if it belongs together. Even the lights have been picked up from sales, although it is always worth having the electrics checked out if you are not an expert.

The circular metal staircase rises to a sleeping area, where there is a double bed tucked into the eaves. It's a limited space, so looks best all in white. The only decoration is a poem beautifully stencilled on the wall behind the bed.

above left and far left: The living area – there is a charming patchwork of different panes of frosted and clear glass in the windows, a legacy of the building's scout-hall days.

top: The snug sleeping platform tucked into the roof space.

above: The cushions on the sofa have been sewn from old Mexican flour sacks.

left: Narrow white shelves on a tiny staircase display objects found on the beach. The pictures are of pressed seaweed, and the shells are arranged in neat lines with similar colours and shapes together.

right: More beachcomber finds, collected over many years of family holidays by the sea. The plain white background provides the perfect setting for their beauty.

VINTAGE DISPLAYS AND COUNTRY COLLECTIONS

Discover the beauty in found objects and everyday things. Group together similar colours and shapes, transforming humble household items into decoration and evoking the memories of childhood holidays.

left: A kitchen range is the focal point for a collection of 1930s and 40s china and cookware.

above: Group similar things together: the shell, gulls' feathers and rope were all found on the local beach.

above right: These are Campari bottles, but you could use jam jars or milk bottles for a similar look – odd-number groupings look better than even ones.

the country kitchen look

The much-loved country kitchen look is one where collections of china and glass are not only on display but also in constant use. Instead of hiding things away behind closed cupboard doors, plates are propped on dressers, mugs hung on hooks and glassware is stacked on open shelves. This kitchen, in the country bolthole of florist Jane Packer, is, as you can see from the gold lettering on the wall above the range cooker, also ideally situated close to the beach.

Jane collects and uses cookware, china and glass from the 1930s and 40s, mixed in with modern items with a similar feel. If you don't want your working dresser to look too cluttered, it's a good idea to choose a theme based on colour or style.

In a kitchen where everything is on show, you need to keep the background simple, especially if the room is also fairly small. Here, a plain window blind instead of a curtain and classic cream kitchen cupboards – made by Jane's father – partnered with white or cream walls make a clean, uncluttered backdrop to her collections.

above and right: Everything in this kitchen is decorative as well as functional, even the vegetables, Kilner storage jars and tea caddies.

Even the most utilitarian item can be pretty – a little pale green vintage vase makes a sweet
holder for the washing-up brush, and even vegetables are treated as still-life decoration,
with fresh radishes and a cabbage arranged in a fruit bowl. Often there's no need to hide
everything away in a fridge – enjoy displaying the colours and shapes of your garden produce.

dresser displays

The back of this kitchen dresser was originally a cheap pine tongue-and-groove, but when painted cream it provides a good background to display plates and mugs. There are pine dressers to be had on every high street, and the look has become something of a country kitchen cliché, but you can paint or stain most dressers to make them look different. If antique dressers are beyond your price range, buy a modern one in a shape or size to suit your kitchen, and then disguise its newness with a coat or two of paint. It's amazing the difference it can make – you can do everything from lacquering a dresser a glossy white or black, to painting it in soft distressed colours, part-painting it as shown here, or staining it to mimic a more expensive wood.

How you arrange the dresser is up to you, but it makes good sense to place precious or less well-used plates and mugs on the top shelves, with the everyday items more easily to hand on the lower shelves. The top of the dresser can also be used to display jugs and vases.

above left: This plate is a piece of contemporary pottery, but its hen theme and pale green background mean it fits into the overall feel.

above: Too many colours in a small house or room make it feel cluttered, so this palette is limited to green, blue and white.

right: The classic country dresser can be painted, part-painted or stained to make it look different from the pine dressers on every high street. Note the simplicity of this one.

These pestles and mortars are used every day, then returned to their shelf. Behind them is a photograph of the same things, creating a lovely echo and a still life with an almost Renaissance-like quality.

using space well

You can use all sorts of corners for displaying collections, from stairwells and windowsills to the narrow spaces between two windows or doors. Here two attractive little wall-hung bookcases have been placed between bedroom doors, and filled with lovely faded books. Old classics or antique leather books are favourites for this kind of treatment, but, in fact even crime or science fiction paperbacks would fit the treatment equally well. Books in a particular genre tend to be packaged in similar ways, which makes them work well in collections – a whole shelf of detective or romantic novels would look equally good.

China is a collectors' area of its own, and many people specialize in particular types, periods or names. There is so much china around that this approach makes a great deal of sense, and it is easier to learn more. Some people choose names like Wedgwood, Goss or Carlton Ware, others are wider in range – blue-and-white is a common one. It makes rummaging in junk shops more fun as your eye will become tuned in to spotting something special, and it gives you confidence that you know what you're buying. There are many books on china marks or makes and many pottery and porcelain factories have been in continuous production for centuries. Focusing on a particular area will make displaying china easier – a collection of blue-and-white china, floral china or work from the 1930s, like Clarice Cliff or Shelley, will automatically look good together.

left: Two pretty little wall-hung bookcases hold a collection of vintage classics by authors such as Jane Austen. This approach would work well with any group of similarly packaged books. The decorative display table below fits perfectly into the small space.

right: Blue-and-white china always looks good together even if it comes from different periods, marks or countries. The key to collecting china is to focus on a theme or name.

left: Splash out on one really good item occasionally – the Chippendale mirror seen here makes everything in the room appear more expensive than it really is.

right: The little wall-hung standing cupboard is an ideal piece for displaying a collection of china birds and animals, and there is also a collection of old postcards by wildlife artist Margaret Tarrant along the top.

In theory every country mantelpiece should house a night-light lantern because power supply can be notoriously erratic in the countryside – in reality, an antique lantern looks good whatever the power situation. Certainly it makes good sense to have an adequate store of candles or night-lights for emergency situations. Collect ways of using candles safely, both indoors and out in the garden on summer evenings – for instance, you could drop night-lights into rinsed-out glass jam jars for a similar effect, and make carrying handles from twisted strands of thick wire.

above: A charming handmade card, a little night-light lantern and seaside 'still life.'

above right: A mantelpiece is always a good place to display collections, such as this grouping of painted china birds. Try changing it completely once or twice a year.

left: This clever wardrobe, used to store fabrics and samples, is a modification of a chainstore unit. It is relatively easy to add extra shelves to the inside of a standard cupboard, giving you exactly the storage you need for hobby or work materials.

right: This upstairs sitting room is used as a study and the table is a working desk, although space is made to display a collection of treasured family photographs – this makes the room seem less office-like. The shelves were originally installed elsewhere in the house. If you do need to take out original fittings in a house, think about whether they can be used elsewhere – shelving can be moved, cupboards cut down and reused, even fireplaces can be taken from one room to another.

left: This 'conservatory' is made from recycled doors and a corrugated plastic roof set onto a simple wooden frame. The doors can be removed entirely in summer if the weather is sufficiently warm. Having hanging baskets of vibrant pelargoniums inside adds to the outdoorsy feel and everything is painted a soft sky blue. The wicker table and iron daybed are both junk-shop finds – you can either paint items like these or leave them fashionably distressed.

right: Blue spotted jugs crammed with country flowers – the more the merrier. Even if you have a city garden, growing traditional blooms will give your patch a country feel.

SUMMER SPACES AND OUTSIDE PLACES

The traditional country-garden look is abundant, colourful and casual. Let the sunshine in by turning even the smallest of courtyards into a haven of light, colour and scent.

PLEASE LEAVE THE
BATTERY AS YOU
WISH TO FIND IT.
ALSO SWEEP
FORECOURT.
(WARDEN)

a room with a view

This sitting room leads out onto decking and then straight down to the beach. You couldn't live any closer to the sea than this! The soft sea blues, greens and greys outside the window are echoed inside the room in the colours of the china, flooring, curtains and the faded chair. The cushions can be used inside or out on the deck. If you have big windows, consider the view outside as inspiration for the scheme inside – a lilac bush in spring, for example, or the acid-green leaves of a lime tree could be the starting point for your colour palette.

left: A seaside palette of cream, white and blue means that the colours inside echo the beach outside – a trick that would work equally for a pretty garden or courtyard view. The floor-length curtains with their hanging 'pelmet' are a good treatment for tall windows.

right: Decking suits painted wooden furniture and deckchair fabrics, and a line of bunting gives a festive feel. You can buy inexpensive softwood garden furniture and paint it in soft whites, blues and greens. Make cushions from brightly coloured scraps of material and decorate with ends of trimming.

weatherproofing

This brick lean-to makes the perfect rustic summerhouse, and, best of all, it has its own fireplace and chimney. An open 'barn' like this makes a brilliant shelter in temperate climates – if you're not sure what the weather is going to do, you can set the table outside yet under shelter, and stoke up the fire if it gets cold. With added bricks and a grill, the fire could also be used as a barbecue, but make sure the chimney is not blocked first. If you're building from scratch, use traditional local bricks and tiles for an authentic effect and design the structure to blend with nearby buildings.

left: This shelter was possibly built as an open log store, but it makes a great place to eat outside, especially with the addition of a fireplace.

below: The old-fashioned watering cans and casual tin table complete the effect, and, during summer evenings, the lean-to can be lit by candlelight.

below: Here, the front door is sufficiently private to be left open on a sunny day. Don't forget areas around the front of the house when you are looking for the best places to sit and enjoy the sun.

right: These pebbles were gathered on long walks and then painted by children on rainy days.

far right: A shower in the garden is unusual, but as the house is near the beach, it has proved useful. There's nothing worse than coming home sandy and walking it into the house.

something different

Sometimes you need to think differently to get the most from your garden. People traditionally sit outside the back door or on terraces next to French windows, but if you have a private space near your front door, that too can turn into a special place with the addition of a little table and a few chairs. In country houses where the front door is hardly ever used and everyone comes in through the back, this can be a way of revitalizing what is often the most attractive part of the house.

It's also the perfect way to enjoy the garden at a different time of day – it's good to be able to have an early breakfast outside when the garden is at its freshest or to enjoy a pre-dinner drink in the evening sun.

Many gardens possess a standpipe, but few go all the way to having a shower outside. Yet if you live in a hot climate or near the sea, a shower in the garden can prevent a lot of mess being taken through the house, and it can also take the pressure off where bathrooms are scarce. But it might not be everyone's idea of bliss on a cold day!

THE PROJECTS

embroidered bed-throw

materials

tracing paper

motif

bed-throw

dressmaker's pins

dressmaker's carbon paper

embroidery hoop

contrast-coloured stranded
cotton embroidery thread

embroidery needle

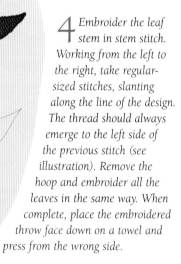

*1 Using the
tracing paper,
trace off the leaf
motif below (or
draw your own).
Mark the leaf
positions on the
throw with pins. Using
the dressmaker's carbon
paper, transfer the design on
to the throw at the pin positions.*

*2 Place one marked
leaf area in an
embroidery hoop and
tighten the screw so
the fabric is taut.*

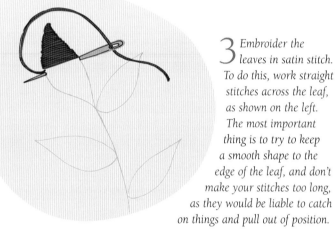

*3 Embroider the
leaves in satin stitch.
To do this, work straight
stitches across the leaf,
as shown on the left.
The most important
thing is to try to keep
a smooth shape to the
edge of the leaf, and don't
make your stitches too long,
as they would be liable to catch
on things and pull out of position.*

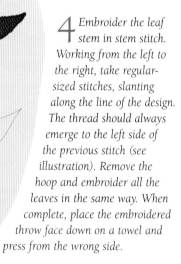

*4 Embroider the leaf
stem in stem stitch.
Working from the left to
the right, take regular-
sized stitches, slanting
along the line of the design.
The thread should always
emerge to the left side of
the previous stitch (see
illustration). Remove the
hoop and embroider all the
leaves in the same way. When
complete, place the embroidered
throw face down on a towel and
press from the wrong side.*

lace-edged napkins

materials

gingham fabric

scissors

iron

sewing machine

contrast-coloured lace

sewing thread

dressmaker's pins

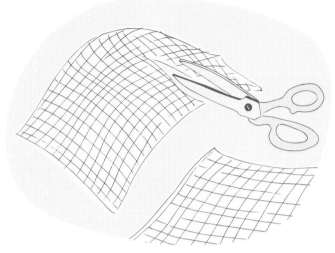

1 *Cut pieces of gingham fabric measuring 42cm (16½in) square.*

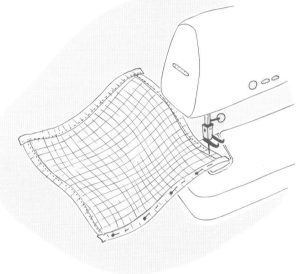

2 *Press a double-turned 1cm (⅜in) hem to the wrong side along each edge of the napkin and machine stitch in place.*

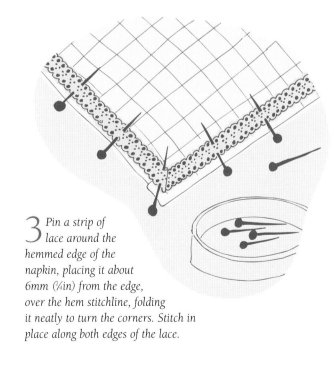

3 *Pin a strip of lace around the hemmed edge of the napkin, placing it about 6mm (¼in) from the edge, over the hem stitchline, folding it neatly to turn the corners. Stitch in place along both edges of the lace.*

Napkins designed by www.stitchdesignworks.co.uk

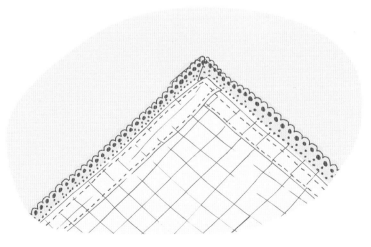

4 *Alternatively, pin the lace so that it extends out beyond the edge of the napkin, folding neatly at the corners and stitch in place along the inner edge of the lace.*

roman blind

materials

tape measure
fabric
lining
scissors
dressmaker's pins
sewing machine
sew and sticky-backed hook-and-loop tape
sewing thread

small plastic rings
2cm (¾in) wooden lath
5 × 2.5cm (2 ×1in) wooden batten
medium-sized screw eyes
nylon blind cord
blind acorn
cleat and screws

1 *Measure the finished width and depth of the blind. Cut out a piece of fabric and lining to the measured width, plus 4cm (1½in) for seams by the depth, plus 12cm (4¾in) for hems.*

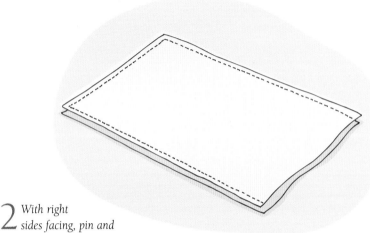

2 *With right sides facing, pin and stitch together the long side edges and top edge of the blind to the lining, with a 2cm (¾in) seam allowance. Clip the corners; turn right side out and press.*

3 *Press the bottom raw edges 2cm (¾in) to the wrong side and then a further 4cm (1½in) to form the casing for the bottom lath. Machine-stitch in place, working close to the first pressed edge.*

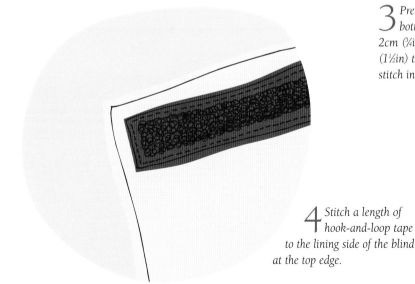

4 *Stitch a length of hook-and-loop tape to the lining side of the blind at the top edge.*

Blind designed by www.sharlandandlewis.com

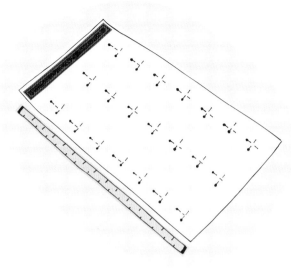

5 On the lining side of the blind,
mark a line down the centre of
the blind using pins. Mark two more
lines 5cm (2in) in from each side
edge of the blind. Starting 15cm
(6in) up from the bottom edge,
mark the ring positions spacing
them at 30cm (12in) intervals
along each pinned line. Leave at
least 20cm (8in) at the top edge
to allow the blind to be raised.
Hand-stitch a small plastic ring to
each position marked along the
lines. Remove all the pins.

6 Slip the lath
into the bottom
casing and slipstitch
the open ends closed.

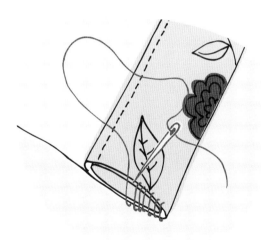

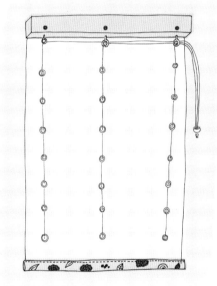

7 Cut the batten to the finished width of blind and paint to
match the wall. Fasten two screw eyes to the underside
of the batten, 5cm (2in) in from ends, with
a third screw eye centrally
between the two. Screw
the batten to the wall
and attach the
sticky side of
hook-and-
loop tape
to the
batten.

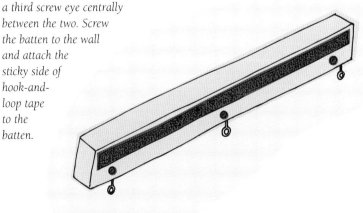

8 With the
blind laid
out flat and the
rings uppermost,
knot a length of cord to each of the bottom rings and
thread the cord vertically up through the rest of the rings.
Attach the blind to the batten with the hook-and-loop
tape. Working from the back of the blind, thread the cords
through the screw eyes above and pass them all across
through the other eyes, so they all pass through the eye
at the operating end. Trim the cords level and attach
the acorn to the ends. Screw the cleat to the side of the
window frame to secure the cords when the blind is raised.

patchwork cushion

materials

variety of cotton fabrics

scissors

tape measure

dressmaker's pins

sewing machine

sewing thread

46cm (18in) cushion pad

1 *From the various fabrics, cut out the pieces for the patchwork front cover: four 22cm (8⅝in) squares and four border strips 49 x 7cm (19¼ x 2¾in). For the back cover, cut two pieces 49 x 35cm (19¼ x 13¾in).*

2 *With right sides facing, stitch two squares together along one side edge, with a 1.5cm (⅝in) seam allowance. Repeat with the remaining two squares. Press seams open.*

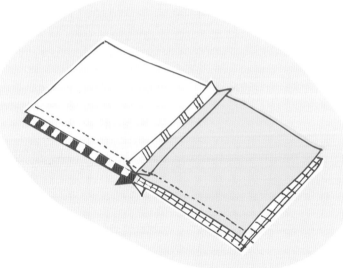

3 *With right sides facing, stitch the two joined square pieces together along one long edge, matching seams and taking a 1.5cm (⅝in) seam turning. Press seam open.*

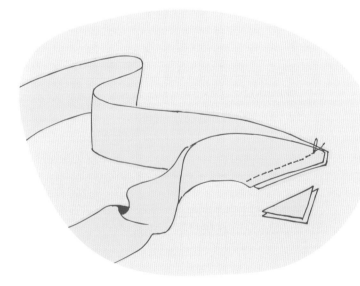

4 *Place one border strip on top of another with right sides facing. Pin and tack the strips together at a 45-degree angle from the top corner, stopping 1.5cm (⅝in) from the bottom edge. Double-check that the angle is correct, then machine-stitch the pieces together along the tacked line. Trim the seams.*

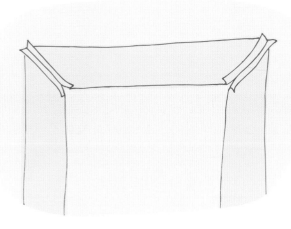

5 *Attach the other strips together in the same way until the border is complete. Press all the seams open.*

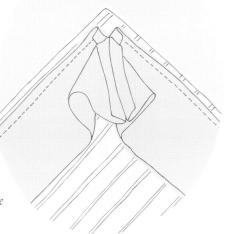

6 *Place the square front panel right side up on a flat surface and pin the border to the outer edge. Stitch in place with a 1.5cm (⅝in) seam allowance. Press the seams open.*

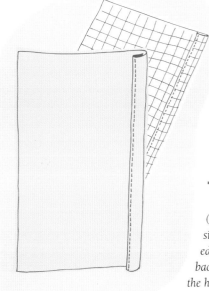

7 *Press a double-turned 12mm (½in) hem to the wrong side down one long edge of each cushion back, and machine-stitch the hems in place.*

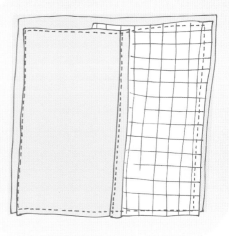

8 *Lay the front cover right side uppermost on a flat surface and place the back panels face down on top, with raw edges level and hemmed edges overlapping at the centre. Machine-stitch the pieces together around the outer edge, with a 1.5cm (⅝in) seam allowance. Trim the corners and turn right side out. Insert the cushion pad through the back opening.*

edging a curtain with antique fabric

materials

ready-made curtains

toning antique fabric

tape measure

scissors

quick un-picker

dressmaker's pins

sewing thread

sewing machine

hand-sewing needle

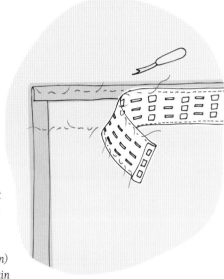

1 *Measure the length of your curtain. Cut a strip of antique fabric for both side edges of the curtain 20cm (8in) wide by the curtain length, plus 4cm (1½in) for hems. Untie the cords on the curtain heading tape and smooth out the gathers. Un-pick the tape for 10cm (4in) at each end.*

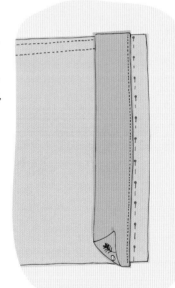

2 *Measure and make a line of pins down the full length of the curtain, 6cm (2⅜in) from the side edge. With right sides facing, lay a fabric strip on the curtain, lining one long edge up with the pin-line and making sure the edges of the strip extend equally at the top and bottom of the curtain. Pin and stitch the strip in place through all layers of fabric, taking a 2cm (¾in) seam allowance.*

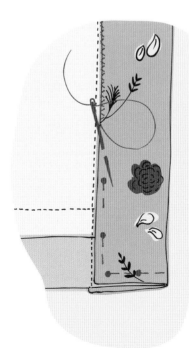

3 *Fold the hem allowance to the wrong side of the curtain at the top and bottom edges and pin in place. Fold the long loose edge of the strip to the wrong side of the curtain, wrapping it closely around the curtain's edge. Fold under the long raw edge of the strip and pin to the reverse of the curtain along the new machine line. Slipstitch the edge in place and the open hem edges together.*

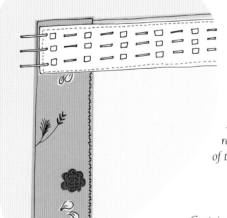

4 *Fold back the heading tape at the top of the curtain and re-stitch in place. Repeat steps 2, 3 and 4 with the remaining side edge of the curtain.*

Curtain idea from www.sharlandandlewis.com

bathroom valance

materials

2cm (¾in) thick plywood

angle brackets

metal eyelets

printed cotton fabric

lining fabric

scissors

tailor's chalk

sewing machine

sewing thread

dressmaker's pins

gathered heading tape

braid trim

curtain hooks

1 *The valance hangs from a pelmet board. Calculate the size and position of your board and attach the angle brackets to the underside of the board. This is now the back edge. Attach the board to the wall above the window and screw eyelets around the edges at regular intervals. Measure the front and sides of the pelmet board and window to calculate the fabric and lining quantities. The valance is slightly gathered so it must be half as wide again as the pelmet board and the depth should be one sixth of the drop from the board to the floor.*

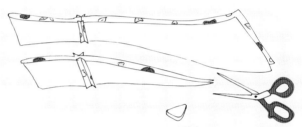

2 *Cut out fabric and lining pieces and join widths if necessary. Fold the lining piece in half, bringing the short edges together and with right sides facing. Using tailor's chalk, shape the bottom edge of the valance so that it curves down at the outer edges. Trim to shape. Trim the fabric piece to match.*

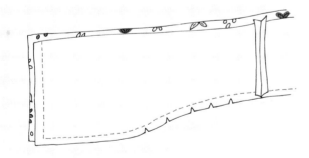

3 *With right sides facing, stitch the fabric and lining pieces together down the side and along the shaped lower edge. Snip curved seam turnings and turn through to the right side; press flat.*

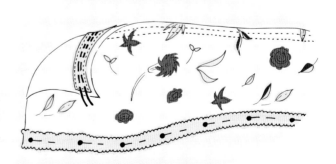

4 *Fold the top edge over 2cm (¾in) to the wrong side. Pin and stitch heading tape to the wrong-side of the top edge. Pin braid to the right side of valance lower-edge and stitch in place. Pull the strings of the heading tape to gather the valance, then knot the ends. Insert as many curtain hooks as there are eyelets on the pelmet board and hang the valance.*

circular tablecloth

materials

tape measure

fabric

scissors

chalk pencil

string

sewing thread

sewing machine

dressmaker's pins

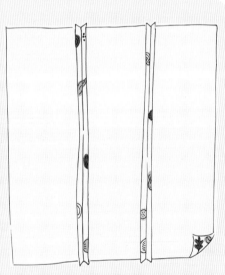

1 *Measure the diameter of your tabletop, deciding on the finished overhang you require. From the overhang measurement, take away 7cm (2¾in) for the depth of the frill. To find your total cloth diameter, double the new overhang measurement and add to the tabletop measurement.*

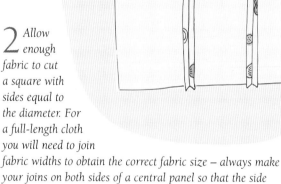

2 *Allow enough fabric to cut a square with sides equal to the diameter. For a full-length cloth you will need to join fabric widths to obtain the correct fabric size – always make your joins on both sides of a central panel so that the side panels are matching widths.*

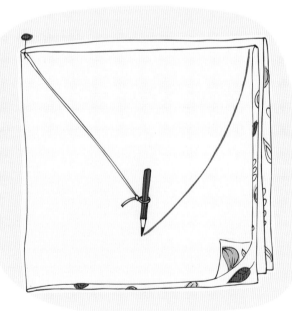

3 *To draw your circular shape, find the radius of your cloth by dividing the diameter in two. With right sides facing, fold your square of fabric into four and draw an arc, using a chalk pencil tied to a length of string; the string should be the radius measurement. Cut along the curved line.*

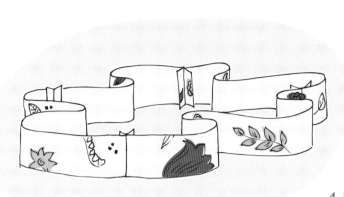

4 For the frill, cut straight-grain strips 16cm (6¼in) wide by 1½–2 times the outer edge of the tablecloth. Join the short ends together to form a continuous circle.

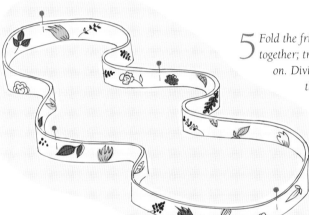

5 Fold the frill in half lengthways, with wrong sides together; treat the double fabric as single from now on. Divide the raw edge of the frill and that of the tablecloth in half and then quarters and mark with pins.

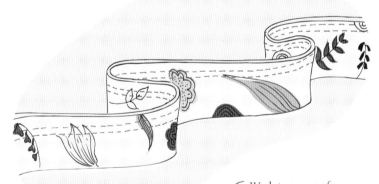

6 Work two rows of gathering stitches (using a long machine stitch) along the raw edge of the frill, placing one row inside the seamline and one row outside. On long edges it is best to work these rows in sections to prevent the threads breaking.

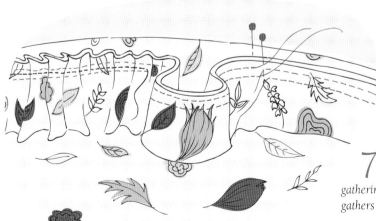

7 With right sides together, pin the frill to the tablecloth edge so that the sections correspond. Pull up the gathering threads so that the frill fits the edge and arrange the gathers evenly. Stitch the frill in place and neaten the raw edges.

re-covering a bar stool

materials

bar stool	piping cord
screwdriver	sewing machine
tape measure	sewing thread
fabric	dressmaker's pins
scissors	staple gun

1 Unscrew the pad from the stool frame and remove the old
cover. Retain the bottom board. If the foam padding is still in
good condition, then reuse it. If not, have a new piece cut to size.

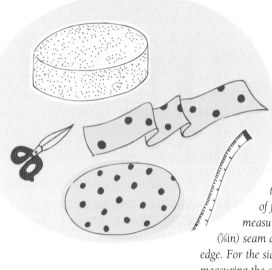

2 Measure the
diameter,
depth and
circumference of
the foam pad. For
the top, cut a circle
of fabric to the diameter
measurement, plus a 1.5cm
(⅝in) seam allowance around the
edge. For the side panel cut out a strip
measuring the circumference of your
pad, by the depth of your pad, adding
4cm (1½in) to each measurement for
seam allowances.

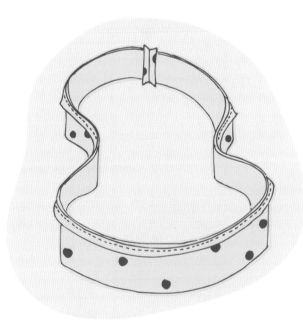

3 Make up
the piping
by cutting a strip of fabric
on the bias, measuring 5cm (2in) by
the same length as your side panel. Place the piping
cord down the centre of the strip on the wrong side.
Bring the long edges of the bias strip together
around the cord and stitch down the length close
to the cord, using a zipper foot on your machine.

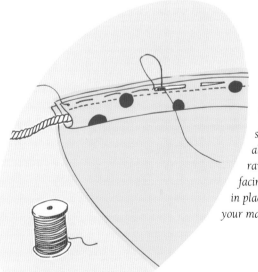

4 Tack the covered
piping to the right
side of the side panel,
along one long edge, with
raw edges level and the cord
facing inwards. Machine-stitch
in place, using a zipper foot on
your machine.

5 With right sides facing, join the short ends of the side panel to
form a circular border, with a 2cm (¾in) seam allowance.

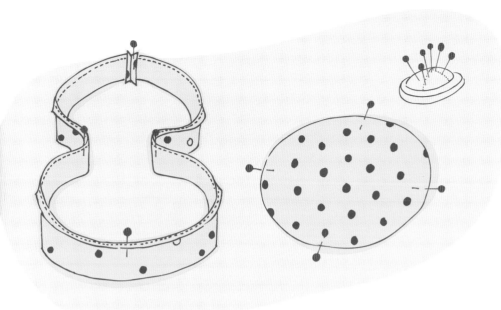

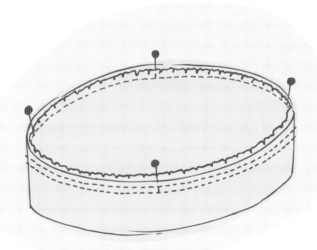

6 Fold the top piece into quarters and mark the quarter positions with pins. Find the quarter points on the piped edge of the circular border and mark the positions with pins.

7 With right sides facing, tack the border to the top piece, matching pins and keeping raw edges level. Machine-stitch the pieces together, working close to the piping cord and using a zipper foot on your machine. Clip seam turnings and turn right side out.

8 Slip the new cover over the foam pad. Insert the bottom board. Fold the overhanging fabric to the underside of the board and fasten in place using a staple gun. Screw the newly covered pad back onto the stool frame.

cork teapot stand

materials

a small side plate

pencil

thin card

craft knife

approximately 60 wine bottle corks

multi-purpose glue, or glue gun

a Jubilee hose clip, approximately 61cm (24in) long

screw driver

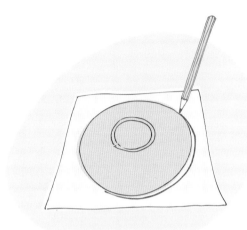

1 *Using the plate as a template, draw a circle onto the thin card and cut out. Mark the central point.*

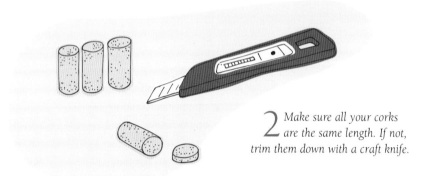

2 *Make sure all your corks are the same length. If not, trim them down with a craft knife.*

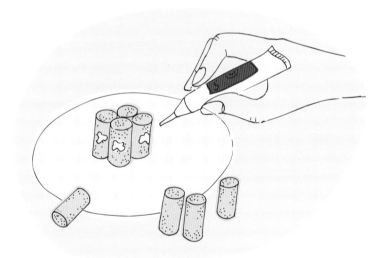

3 *Stand the first cork end up, in the centre of the card circle. Place a circle of corks around the central cork, using a spot of glue to stick their sides together. Do not stick to the card circle. Continue sticking corks around the central core until the cardboard circle is covered. Leave to dry fully overnight (unless using a glue gun).*

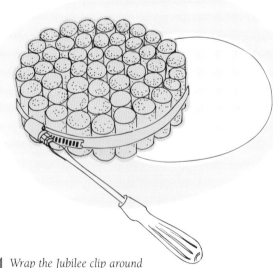

4 *Wrap the Jubilee clip around the corks and thread the end into the fastener. Using a screwdriver, tighten up the clip to bind the corks tightly together and lift off the card template.*

gilding a mirror

materials

framed mirror

methylated spirits

acrylic paint

matt medium

1 flat brush for paint, size and varnish

size

transfer gold leaf

1 broad soft-hair brush

1 bristle brush

fine-grade wire wool (optional)

shellac varnish

brush cleaner

1 Remove the mirror from the frame. If your frame has previously been painted or varnished, give it a light sanding and a good clean with methylated spirits, unless the paint is thick, uneven, or chipped. In this case, the piece needs to be thoroughly stripped and sealed.

2 After preparing the surface, apply two coats of acrylic paint for a basecoat, diluting it with a matt medium so that the finish is less shiny. Leave to dry thoroughly.

3 Evenly apply a thin coat of size to the frame and leave to dry for approximately 15 minutes until it turns clear and tacky. The size will remain tacky for some time. Once tacky, place a sheet of gold leaf on the frame and brush it gently into place with the soft brush, remove the tissue backing-paper. Lay the next sheet of leaf down so that it overlaps slightly, and repeat until the entire surface is covered. When applying to raised surfaces, you may need to use small pieces of leaf to fill in the crevices first, using the soft brush to tap it into the grooves. Use the bristle brush to remove any overhanging pieces.

4 For an aged look, leave the frame to dry for a couple of days, then rub it down with a fine-grade wire wool to revel the base colour in places. Finally, seal with shellac varnish and leave to dry. Replace the mirror.

ADDRESSES

20TH-CENTURY ANTIQUES AND VINTAGE FABRICS

SHARLAND AND LEWIS
Decorative antiques from
France and England
www.sharlandandlewis.com
01666 500354

HOPSCOTCH QUILTS
Make-your-own patchwork
quilting sets using recycled
and vintage materials
www.hopscotchquilts.co.uk
07788 662619

HOUSEPOINTS
Affordably priced country
furniture
18a Preston Street, Faversham
Kent ME13 8NZ
01795 530900

FABRICS AND HOMEWARES

STITCH DESIGNWORKS
Contemporary home and
lifestyle store selling colourful
natural fabrics and furniture
www.stitchdesignworks.co.uk

CATH KIDSTON
Vintage-style fabrics and
furniture
www.cathkidston.co.uk
0845 026 2440

KAFFE FASSETT
Designer of patchwork,
knitwear and needlework
www.kaffefassett.com

WOOD AND MDF FURNITURE SUPPLIED TO PAINT

SCUMBLE GOOSIE
www.scumble-goosie.co.uk

DORMY HOUSE
www.thedormyhouse.com
01264 365808

KITCHENS

NICK KENNY
Kitchens and recycled
furniture
01795 538898

HISTORIC PAINTS

PAINT AND PAPER LIBRARY
www.paintlibrary.co.uk
0207823 7755

PAPERS & PAINTS
www.papers-paints.co.uk
020 7352 8626

FARROW & BALL
www.farrow-ball.com
01202 876141

HOUSE RENOVATION AND MAINTENANCE

THE SOCIETY FOR THE PROTECTION OF ANCIENT BUILDINGS
Courses and technical advice
for owners of period homes
www.spab.org.uk
020 7377 1644

THE BUILDINGS CONSERVATION DIRECTORY
Listings of traditional and
historic materials, craftsmen
and companies
www.buildingconservation.com
01747 871717

SALVO
International directory of
architectural salvage and
antique dealers with code of
practice to avoid stolen
goods. Also includes directory
of repro and replica fixtures
and fittings
www.salvo.com

MISCELLANEOUS

JANE PACKER
Flowers
www.janepackerdelivered.com
0845 0746000

SAMWAYS FARM
Bed & Breakfast
Alvediston
Salisbury
Wiltshire SP5 5LQ
www.samwaysfarm.co.uk
01722 780286

JULIA DICKENS
Watercolour artist in
Hindhead, Surrey
01428 605729

THE BATTERY
Home on the beach (pages
84–93) available as
photographic location
www.jjlocations.co.uk

INDEX

ACKNOWLEDGEMENTS

A huge thank you to Simon Brown whose stunning photographs captured the spirit of this book so brilliantly. Thank you to dear friends who let us photograph their homes and to the lovely new people we met who welcomed us into their houses, and thank you to the team at Cico Books: Cindy Richards – the driving force behind the book – Sally Powell, Gillian Haslam and, of course, Christine Wood for the invaluable design work.